Fact Finders™

Questions and Answers: Countries

Costa Rica

A Question and Answer Book

by Mary Englar

Consultant:
Colin M. MacLachlan
John Christy Barr Distinguished Professor of History
Tulane University
New Orleans, Louisiana

Capstone
press

Mankato, Minnesota

Fact Finders is published by Capstone Press,
151 Good Counsel Drive, P.O. Box 669, Mankato, Minnesota 56002.
www.capstonepress.com

Library of Congress Cataloging-in-Publication Data
Englar, Mary.
    Costa Rica : a question and answer book / by Mary Englar.
Summary: "Describes the geography, history, economy, and culture of Costa Rica in a
    question-and-answer format"–Provided by publisher.
    p. cm.—(Fact finders. Questions and answers. Countries)
    Includes bibliographical references and index.
    ISBN 0–7368–4352–3 (hardcover)
    1. Costa Rica—Juvenile literature. I. Title. II. Series.
F1543.2.E54 2006
972.86—dc22   2005001162

Editorial Credits

Silver Editions, editorial, design, and production; Kia Adams, set designer; Ortelius Design,
Inc., cartographer; Wanda Winch, photo researcher; Scott Thoms, photo editor

Photo Credits

Beryl Goldberg, 13; Cory Langley, 21, 25; DigitalVision/Gerry Ellis, 1; Houserstock/Ellen
Barone, 4; Houserstock/Michael J. Pettypool, cover (background); Index Stock
Imagery/HIRB, cover (foreground), 16–17; Index Stock Imagery/Inga Spence, 27; Kevin
Schafer Photography, 12; One Mile Up, Inc., 29 (flag); Photo Courtesy of the Asamblea
Legislativa De Costa Rica, 8–9; Photo Courtesy of El Museo Nacional del Jade Fidel Tristán
Castro, San Jose, Costa Rica, 20; Photo Courtesy of Paul Baker, 29 (coins); Photo Courtesy of
Richard Sutherland, 29 (bill); Phottri-MicroStock, 18–19; South American Pictures/Robert
Francis, 10–11, 15; The Granger Collection, New York, 7; The Image
Works/HAGA/Tsuyoshi Kishimoto, 22–23

Artistic Effects:

Comstock, 24

1 2 3 4 5 6 10 09 08 07 06 05

Table of Contents

Features

Where is Costa Rica?

Costa Rica is in Central America. It is a little smaller than West Virginia.

Mountains cover much of Costa Rica. A central mountain **plateau** has rich soil and a cool climate. The Pacific coast is rocky. The Caribbean coast is hot and rainy. Forests along the coasts have more than 100 kinds of trees.

Coffee plants grow well on the slopes of the Monteverde Cloud Forest.

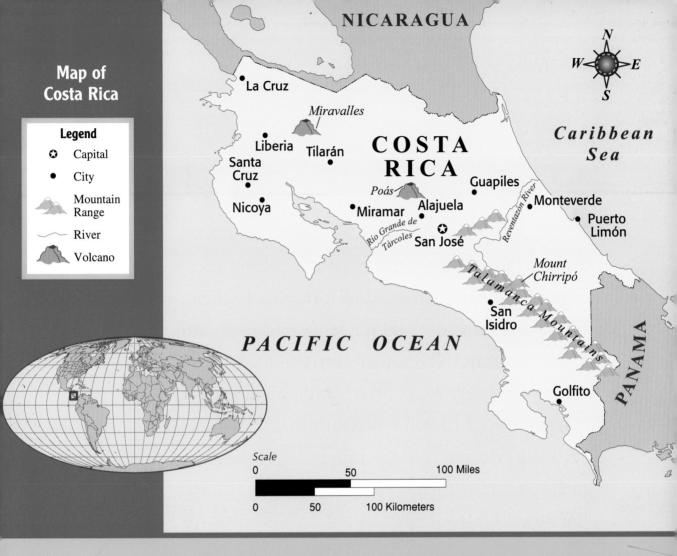

Map of Costa Rica

Legend
- ✪ Capital
- • City
- 🏔 Mountain Range
- 〜 River
- 🌋 Volcano

NICARAGUA

La Cruz

Miravalles

Liberia Tilarán

COSTA RICA

Santa Cruz

Poás

Guapiles

Nicoya

Miramar Alajuela

Río Grande de Tárcoles

San José

Reventazón River

Monteverde

Puerto Limón

Caribbean Sea

Mount Chirripó

Talamanca Mountains

San Isidro

PACIFIC OCEAN

Golfito

PANAMA

Scale
0   50   100 Miles
0   50   100 Kilometers

In the past, forests covered most of Costa Rica. But people cut down many forests for farmland. Now, Costa Rica protects its forests and wildlife. Many birds, snakes, frogs, monkeys, and other animals live in the 23 national parks.

When did Costa Rica become a country?

In the 1500s, Spanish explorers came to Costa Rica. Costa Rica became a **colony** of Spain. The Spanish tried to force Costa Rican Indians to work for them. Most of the Indians escaped from the Spanish into the forests.

In the early 1800s, the Spanish colony of Mexico fought for its freedom from Spain. In 1821, Mexico declared its independence from Spain. It formed an empire that included Costa Rica.

Fact!

The Chorotega were the most powerful group of Indians in Costa Rica when the Spanish arrived.

Agustín Iturbide led the fight against Spain for Mexican independence. In 1821, he rode his horse into Mexico City with his army.

Agustín Iturbide became the emperor. The empire broke up in 1823. Costa Rica then became an **independent** country.

What type of government does Costa Rica have?

Costa Rica's government is a **democratic republic**. Every four years, Costa Ricans vote for new leaders. All Costa Ricans age 18 and older must vote. The government can fine anyone who does not vote.

The people vote for a president and two vice presidents. The president is the head of the government.

Fact!

Costa Rica does not have an army. The people are proud of their peaceful history.

The 57 members of the Legislative Assembly serve a four-year term.

The people also vote for members of the Legislative Assembly. The Assembly makes the country's laws. It is similar to the U.S. Congress. The Assembly meets in the National Palace in San José, the capital city.

What kind of housing does Costa Rica have?

Most Costa Ricans live in houses. City houses have cement-block walls and iron roofs. Rural houses have either cement or wood walls. Most rural houses have a front porch. Families can sit together and talk with neighbors. Costa Ricans often paint their houses bright pink, green, or blue.

Where do people in Costa Rica live?

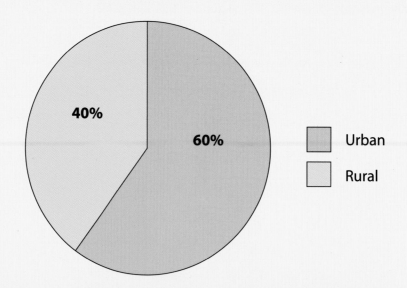

40%

60%

Urban

Rural

Some poor neighborhoods in San José are crowded with houses.

Costa Rica does not have enough housing for everyone. Many large cities have this problem. Some people build houses with old wood and iron. The houses do not have water or electricity. The people in these neighborhoods are very poor.

What are Costa Rica's forms of transportation?

Costa Rica has many kinds of transportation. Cars, trucks, and buses share the narrow city streets. Many people take the bus to work.

Most people also travel by bus between towns. In the mountains, the roads are mostly dirt. In some areas, people still ride horses from place to place.

Tourists travel by water taxi on a canal in Tortuguero National Park.

Streets in large cities are often filled with long lines of cars and buses.

Much of the Caribbean coast is swampy. The government dug a **canal** to connect the port cities. Water taxis carry people through the wetlands. Farmers take bananas to market in canoes with motors.

What are Costa Rica's major industries?

Most people in Costa Rica work in **service industries**. They work in schools, government offices, and hospitals. Costa Rica's national parks attract many visitors every year. Costa Ricans work in parks, hotels, and restaurants.

In the rural areas, most people are farmers. They grow coffee, bananas, sugarcane, and pineapples. Many bananas sold in the United States come from Costa Rica. Ranchers in the northwest raise cattle.

What does Costa Rica import and export?

Imports	Exports
consumer goods	bananas
electronics	beef
equipment	cocoa

Workers on banana plantations sort bananas with the help of machines.

Other Costa Ricans work in factories. Many prepare food or sew clothing. A large computer chip company built a factory in Costa Rica in 1998. Computer factories provide many new jobs.

What is school like in Costa Rica?

School is free for all children from grade school through high school. Children between ages 7 and 13 must go to school. The school year lasts from March to November.

In the cities, classes in public schools are large. Some parents pay for their children to go to private schools.

Fact!

Some students live and go to school in a cloud forest. This kind of rain forest is in the mountains where clouds cover the forest most of the time. Every day students learn about animals in the cloud forest. Then they take a hike to see them.

Students in Costa Rica go to school for nine months of the year.

In the rural areas, many students go to a one-room schoolhouse. Students of all ages study together. Some rural schools only have a few books. Teachers must make copies of the books for their students.

What are Costa Rica's favorite sports and games?

Soccer is Costa Rica's favorite sport. Soccer is called *fútbol* in Spanish. Every small town has a soccer field. People get very excited when they watch their favorite team. If their team wins, fans honk their car horns.

Fact!

Claudia Poll won the first Olympic gold medal for Costa Rica. In 1996, she won a gold medal in swimming.

Surfing in the Pacific Ocean is a popular sport.

Good beaches line both coasts. Many families swim and fish during school holidays. **Surfing** became popular in the 1990s. Some surfers live on the Pacific coast beaches. They surf the biggest waves early in the morning.

What are the traditional art forms in Costa Rica?

Costa Rica's national symbol is a painted oxcart. In the past, farmers filled the carts with coffee beans. Oxen pulled the carts to market. Bright red, orange, and yellow designs covered the carts. Today, artists still paint small oxcarts for parades and for tourists.

Fact!

The Jade Museum in San José has jade carvings. Costa Rica's Indians carved the green stones into jaguars, monkeys, and frogs.

Painting oxcarts is a tradition that is more than one hundred years old.

In northwest Costa Rica, the **descendants** of the Chorotega Indians make pottery by hand. These artists respect nature. They paint lizards, bats, or jaguars on their pots. The potters teach their children to make pottery. They also teach the grade-school children in their villages.

What major holidays do Costa Ricans celebrate?

Every town in Costa Rica holds a festival every year. Sometimes the festivals honor Catholic saints. Other festivals raise money for a church, school, or hospital. Many festivals include giant masked clowns. People enjoy games, parades, and music.

Costa Ricans celebrate Independence Day on September 15. Children all over Costa Rica dress up and take part in parades.

What other holidays do people in Costa Rica celebrate?

Day of the Dead
Easter
Independence Day
Labor Day
Mother's Day
New Year's Day

To celebrate Independence Day, girls dress in costumes for a parade. Their sashes tell which town they come from.

Most Costa Ricans celebrate the Roman Catholic holidays. For Christmas, families decorate their homes with colored lights. The children write to the Christ child to ask for presents. Families set up small statues of Mary, Joseph, and baby Jesus.

What are the traditional foods of Costa Rica?

Most Costa Ricans eat black beans and rice with every meal. The traditional breakfast of rice and beans is called *gallo pinto*. Sometimes eggs, tortillas, and sour cream are added. Other meals include beef or chicken with rice and beans.

Fact!

Costa Rica grows the second largest crop of bananas in the world. Only Ecuador grows more.

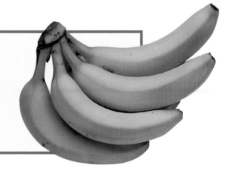

Many Costa Ricans sell fruit drinks and snacks from colorful stands.

In most cities, Costa Ricans sell sweets from a street stand. Coconut cakes, fudge, and roasted bananas are popular snacks. Many people like cold drinks made from bananas, pineapples, or strawberries. The fruit is mixed with ice and milk.

What is family life like in Costa Rica?

In the past, people stayed in their home villages. Now, young people move to the cities for good jobs. On Sundays and holidays, people return to their home villages. They go to parks or visit with their families.

What are the ethnic backgrounds of people in Costa Rica?

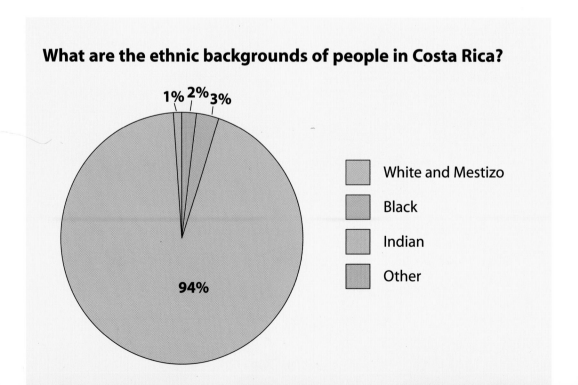

- White and Mestizo
- Black
- Indian
- Other

Most Costa Rican mothers go shopping for food for their family.

Most women do not work outside the home. They take care of their children. They also clean the house and cook. On farms, both mothers and fathers work. Boys feed the animals and help in the fields. Girls clean the house and take care of younger children.

Costa Rica Fast Facts

Official name:

Republic of Costa Rica

Population:

3,956,507 people

Land area:

19,714 square miles
(51,060 square kilometers)

Capital city:

San José

Average annual precipitation:

74 inches (188 centimeters)

Language:

Spanish

Average January temperature (San José):

66 degrees Fahrenheit
(19 degrees Celsius)

Natural resources:

fisheries, forests,
hydroelectric power

Average July temperature (San José):

69 degrees Fahrenheit
(21 degrees Celsius)

Religions:

Roman Catholic	76%
Protestant	16%
Other	8%

Money and Flag

Money:

Costa Rica's money is the colón. In 2005, one U.S. dollar equaled 465 colónes. One Canadian dollar equaled 374 colónes.

Flag:

The Costa Rican flag has five stripes. The coat of arms is in the red stripe. The seven stars in the coat of arms represent Costa Rica's seven provinces.

Learn to Speak Spanish

Costa Rica's official language is Spanish. Learn to speak some Spanish words using the chart below.

English	Spanish	Pronunciation
good morning	buenos días	(BWAY-nohs DEE-ahs)
good-bye	adiós	(ah-dee-OHS)
please	por favor	(POR fah-VOR)
thank you	gracias	(GRAH-see-us)
yes	sí	(SEE)
no	no	(NO)
How are you?	¿Cómo estás?	(KOH-moh ay-STAHS)
Costa Ricans	Ticos	(TEE-kohs)

Glossary

canal (kuh-NAL)—a channel dug across land and filled with water so boats can carry people and products

colony (KOL-uh-nee)—an area that is settled by people from another country and that is ruled by that country

democratic republic (dem-uh-KRAT-ik ri-PUHB-lik)—a government in which the people vote for their leaders

descendants (di-SEND-uhnts)—your children, their children and so on into the future

independent (in-di-PEN-duhnt)—free from the control of other people or things

plateau (pla-TOH)—area of high, flat land

service industries (SUR-viss IN-duh-streez)—businesses that help and take care of customers

surfing (SURF-ing)—using a board to ride on waves

Internet Sites

FactHound offers a safe, fun way to find Internet sites related to this book. All of the sites on FactHound have been researched by our staff.

Here's how:
1. Visit *www.facthound.com*
2. Type in this special code **0736843523** for age-appropriate sites. Or enter a search word related to this book for a more general search.
3. Click on the **Fetch It** button.

FactHound will fetch the best sites for you!

Read More

Deady, Kathleen W. *Costa Rica.* A True Book. New York: Children's Press, 2004.

Fox, Mary Virginia. *Costa Rica.* A Visit To. Chicago: Heinemann Library, 2001.

Garrett, Rosalie and Nicole Frank. *Welcome to Costa Rica.* Welcome to My Country. Milwaukee: Gareth Stevens, 2001.

Streissguth, Thomas. *Costa Rica in Pictures.* Visual Geography Series. Minneapolis: Lerner, 2005.

Index